W9-BZW-991

結界師
KEKKAISHI
5
田辺イエロウ
YELLOW TANABE PRESENTS

The Story Thus Far

Yoshimori Sumimura and Tokine Yukimura have a special mission, passed down through their families for generations. Their mission is to protect Karasumori forest from supernatural beings called *ayakashi*. People with this gift for terminating ayakashi are called *kekkaishi*, or barrier masters.

Yoshimori has come up with a grand scheme to seal off the power of Karasumori forever. In order to accomplish this impossible task, he must not only train and perfect his skills but also delve into the mystery surrounding his ancestral lands.

KEKKAISHI VOL. 5

TABLE OF CONTENTS

Chapter 36: What Is Karasumori?

WHAT IS KARASUMORI ?
THE MORE I THINK ABOUT IT, THE MORE CONFUSED I GET...
I ASKED MADARAO ABOUT IT YESTERDAY...
WHAT IS KARASUMORI?
IT'S THE NAME OF THE LORD WHO RULED THIS AREA A LONG TIME AGO.
NO ...
I MEAN WHAT EXACTLY IS THE POWER OF KARASUMORI?
WHO KNOWS ?
...
HEY...
WHAT ABOUT THE STORY OF THE UNDERGROUND SHRINE DEDICATED TO THE LORD? IS THAT TRUE?

THE SHRINE IS...
...LARGELY, IF NOT ENTIRELY, SEALED OFF BY KEKKAI, RIGHT?
PROB-ABLY.
PROB-ABLY?
School
Shrine
Kekkai
WHO CREATED THE KEKKAI AND HOW DID HE DO IT?
I GUESS ONE OF YOUR ANCESTORS DID IT SOMEHOW
HEY, WAIT A MINUTE.
YOU'VE BEEN A DEMON DOG SINCE THAT TIME.
YOU MUST KNOW WHO DID IT.
I GUESS YOU'RE RIGHT.
BUT IT HAPPENED SO LONG AGO...
WHO KNOWS IF THE OLD STORIES THAT HAVE BEEN HANDED DOWN ARE ACCURATE OR NOT.
AND THAT USELESS DEMON DOG CAN'T REMEMBER ANYTHING ABOUT IT.
NONE OF THE SCROLLS OF KEKKAI TEACHINGS HAVE MUCH TO SAY ABOUT KARASUMORI EITHER.
YAWN

SKRATCH
SKRATCH
I WISH I HAD ASKED MASAMORI ABOUT IT.
I COULD ASK GRANDPA, BUT I'LL HAVE TO BE PREPARED FOR HIS WRATH.
TAP
TAP TAP
I WONDER IF TOKINE KNOWS ANYTHING ABOUT IT?
NO, I SHOULDN'T ASK HER.
DON'T WANT TO INVOLVE HER. THIS COULD BE DANGEROUS.
HEY, SUMIMURA. ARE YOU ALL RIGHT?
DARN IT! I'M SLEEPY AND CONFUSED. WHAT THE HECK?!
SKRATCH SKRATCH
HE'S ANGRY BECAUSE HE'S SLEEPY?

YOU'RE KIDDING!
GET SOME SLEEP.
MMM.
SUMIMURA? THAT DULL GUY?
I DON'T UNDERSTAND YOUR TASTE, YURI.
WHAT'S SO APPEALING ABOUT HIM?
GASP!
DON'T MISUNDERSTAND ME, KYOKO!
I...I DIDN'T MEAN TO SAY I LIKE HIM. I'M JUST CURIOUS ABOUT HIM...
PANIC ATTACK
OH NO!
WHAT ARE YOU CURIOUS ABOUT?
UM... WELL ...
YOU SEE...
I GUESS I SHOULDN'T TALK ABOUT HIS POWERS.
DON'T TELL ANYBODY ABOUT THIS, OKAY?
I PROMISED I'D KEEP IT A SECRET.

HOW CAN I EXPLAIN WITHOUT TALKING ABOUT HIS POWERS?
Yuri's Brain is churning.
SPIN SPIN SPIN SPIN SPIN
H_2O
apple
GLARE
SLUMP
SORRY ...I CAN'T EXPLAIN.
THERE'S NOTHING INTER-ESTING ABOUT HIM.
HE'S ALWAYS ASLEEP AND HE JUST DOESN'T STAND OUT.
HE'S NOT PARTICULARLY A GOOD STUDENT OR GOOD ATHLETE. HE'S NOT GOOD LOOKING AND HE'S SHORT.
BUT...
HE'S TALLER THAN ME!
OH, I SEE. YOU'RE DRAWN TO ORDINARY GUYS?
BUT HE'S THE FURTHEST THING FROM ORDINARY...
HUH?
THIS IS GREAT!
YOUR CHANCES ARE BETTER WITH AN ORDINARY GUY!
WHAT DO YOU MEAN?
GO FOR IT, YURI!
GO TALK TO HIM!
BE BRAVE!
CLENCH
WHAT?
BE BRAVE?

TALK TO HIM ABOUT WHAT?
WHATEVER!
MAYBE YOU GUYS SHARE A COMMON INTEREST AND THAT WOULD BE GREAT!
A COMMON INTEREST?
I KNOW WE HAVE A COMMON INTEREST...
YOU KNOW THAT ALREADY?
WHY DON'T YOU USE IT TO PURSUE HIM?
SPIRITS AND STUFF.
BUT IT'S NOT A FUN SUBJECT...
WHAT ARE YOU TALKING ABOUT?
BUZZ
BUZZ
GEEZ.
I WISH I HADN'T BROUGHT THIS UP...
TK
TK

EEK.
WHO IS THAT MAN? I WONDER IF HE'S...
SPLASH
I WONDER IF HE'S A GHOST...
I'M STARTING TO SEE MORE AND MORE GHOSTS SINCE I ENROLLED IN THIS SCHOOL.
SKWK
...

UM.
EXCUSE ME!
MMM?
FWMP
MUSS
KANDA?
RUB
RUB
WHAT'S UP?
UH... UM...
I WANT TO ASK...
...YOUR OPINION ABOUT SOME-THING.
WOW! LOOK AT YURI.
SHE'S ALREADY GOING INTO ACTION!
GO FOR IT!
...

RUB
WHISPER
YOU MEAN SOMETHING ABOUT GHOSTS?
YES...
LET'S TALK ABOUT IT DURING THE NEXT BREAK.
WHAT HAPPENED.
DID YOU SEE SOME-THING?
YES, BUT WHAT I WANTED TO ASK YOU IS...
...IF THERE'S ANY WAY TO STOP SEEING GHOSTS.
CAN I MAKE IT STOP?

HMM ... I DON'T KNOW.
YOU DON'T KNOW?
DOES SEEING GHOSTS BOTHER YOU?
OF COURSE!
SNEAK
I'M SURPRISED SHE'S DOING THIS.
SHE ASKED HIM TO GO UP TO THE ROOF!
KYAA
I WONDER IF THIS IS A GOOD IDEA.
I GET SCARED AND...
THEY USUALLY WON'T HARM YOU UNLESS YOU REACT TO THEM IN A WEIRD WAY.
JUST IGNORE THEM.
HOW CAN I IGNORE THEM?!
IT'S BETTER NOT TO LET YOURSELF GET TOO SCARED OF THEM.
BUT...
BUT I CAN'T TELL...
I CAN'T TELL THE DIFFERENCE BETWEEN HUMANS AND GHOSTS.
WHAT?

WELL...
CAN'T YOU TELL FROM THE WAY THEY LOOK?
NO, I CAN'T!
HOW DO YOU TELL THE DIFFERENCE?
THAT IS A PROBLEM.
UH-OH...
HE SEEMS TROUBLED BY HER CONFESSION OF LOVE.
NO WAY! DID SHE ALREADY TELL HIM ABOUT HER FEELINGS?
I CAN'T HEAR THEM.
RECENTLY I'VE BEEN SEEING A MAN IN A KIMONO AT SCHOOL FROM TIME TO TIME.
HE'S A GHOST, ISN'T HE?
A MAN IN A KIMONO?
THAT DOES SOUND LIKE A GHOST.
IS IT ALWAYS THE SAME GUY?
I DON'T THINK SO. I THINK THERE ARE SEVERAL OF THEM.
I SAW ONE JUST A FEW MINUTES AGO...
...NEAR THE FLOWERBEDS IN BACK.
OH! THERE HE IS!
DASH
YOSHIMORI!
WAH! HE'S RUNNING TOWARD US!
OH NO!

DASH
DASH
DASH
WHAT'S THAT ALL ABOUT?
HE RAN AWAY FROM YURI...
DASH
DASH
DASH
SKID
SKID
DASH
DASH
DASH
STOP RIGHT THERE!

WHAT ARE YOU DOING HERE?
...GEN-SAN?
OH?
WHAT'S UP, YOSHI? YOU ARE DRESSED LIKE A JUNIOR HIGH STUDENT.
OH.
I AM A JUNIOR HIGH STUDENT. WHAT ARE YOU DOING HERE?
WELL, I DON'T LIKE THE WAY THIS BRANCH LOOKS...
EXCUSE ME, BUT THESE TREES BELONG TO THE SCHOOL.
GLARE
YOU'RE NOT ALLOWED TO CUT THEM.
WHAT ARE YOU TALKING ABOUT? WHO COULD IGNORE SUCH AN UNRULY LOOKING BRANCH?
WHAT?
SNIP
YOU'RE A GONER!
PLEASE JUST GO HOME!
IF SOMEONE SEES YOU WITH THOSE CLIPPERS, THEY MIGHT CALL THE POLICE!
PLEASE?

HUFF
HUFF
YOSHIMORI CAME BACK IN SUCH A RUSH. HE'S OUT OF BREATH.
I WONDER IF HE'S MADE UP HIS MIND ABOUT YURI.
THE MAN IN KIMONO YOU JUST SAW IS JUST A GUY WHO LIVES AROUND HERE.
HUFF
HUFF
HE SOMETIMES SHOWS UP AT THE SCHOOL-YARD TO TRIM THE TREES.
HE'S NOT A BAD GUY.
ANYWAY ...
...IF YOU NOTICE ANYONE WHO LOOKS STRANGE, JUST STAY AWAY FROM HIM.
DON'T WORRY.
I'LL TAKE CARE OF TERMINATING ANY BAD GUYS THAT TURN UP.
DO YOU FEEL BETTER NOW?

YES, I DO. THANKS, YOSHIMORI.
WOW!
IT LOOKS LIKE THINGS ARE WORKING OUT FOR THEM!
ARE YOU SURE?
I'M GLAD I TALKED TO HIM.
TKTK
GIGGLE
I FEEL BETTER NOW.
OH.
ANOTHER MAN IN A KIMONO...
BUT I'M JUST GOING TO IGNORE IT THIS TIME!

It's been a while...
BOINNG

XAVIER ITO THE ETHICS TEACHER IS A BIG PAIN.
HA HA HA
SHF
I'M SERIOUS.
HUH?
WHAT?
WHERE'D MY PASTRY GO?!
MAYBE YOU FINISHED IT WITHOUT REALIZING IT?
NO WAY...
I COULDN'T HAVE!
I SWEAR I ONLY HAD ONE BITE!
CHOMP
CHOMP
TELL HIM I LIKE HIM?
YOU MEAN DIDN'T TELL HIM?
ZZZ

Chapter 37:
Lord Uro

WHAT'S WRONG?
MY CHICKEN DIS-APPEARED...
MUNCH MUNCH
DIDN'T YOU JUST EAT IT?
MAYBE YOU DROPPED IT.
HEY!
WHO DID IT?
WHO DRANK MY JUICE?
SLURP
MY SHRIMP!
WH AM
WH AM
MY EGGS!
MY JUMBO PASTRY!
Jumbo Pastry
WHAM

AT THE CAFETERIA
CHATTER
CHATTER
MA'AM, ARE YOU OUT OF YAKI SOBA BREAD?
IF YOU DON'T SEE ANY THERE, THEN WE'RE OUT OF THEM.
LOOK CAREFULLY.
HMM ...
I GUESS YOU'RE OUT...
RUSTLE
RUSTLE
RUSTLE
OH.
I FOUND THIS EMPTY BAG.
WHAT?
FLAP
MUNCH
!
DON
SMILE

MA'AM, YOU'RE ALL OUT.
RUSTLE
RUSTLE
PLOP
牛乳
MILK
WHAT'S WRONG, TOKINE?
I JUST REMEMBERED SOMETHING!
TAK TAK TAK TAK
TAK
SO FAST!
SLUUURP
SORRY, GOTTA GO!
TOKINE?!
DASH

AH!
BUMP
SORRY!
OUCH!
I LOST HIM?
BUT IT'S STRANGE... NORMALLY, I IMMEDIATELY SENSE WHEN AYAKASHI ENTER THE SCHOOL GROUNDS.
JUNIOR HIGH SECTION
BUZZ
BUZZ
HA HA HA
USUALLY I WOULD BE RELISHING THIS LUNCH, BUT...
I'M TOO SLEEPY TODAY.
MUNCH
MUNCH

I'M GOING TO HAVE TO GO TO MY SECRET SPOT FOR A NAP FOR THE REST OF LUNCH.
SHF
SHF
SHF
KLANK
HEY, SUMIMURA. WHERE ARE YOU GOING?
DASH
RESTROOM!
RATTLE
HE'S GONE ...?
WAS IT JUST AN ILLUSION?
MAYBE I WAS DREAMING?
RUB RUB

SLAM
RATTLE
SUMIMURA? DIDN'T YOU NEED TO GO TO THE RESTROOM?
WELL, MAYBE I SHOULD IGNORE IT. I DIDN'T SENSE ANYTHING EVIL.
CHANGED MY MIND.
BUZZ
TP
CLICK
BUZZ
THERE'S NOTHING AMISS IN THE HIGH SCHOOL SECTION.
I WANT TO CHECK OUT THE JUNIOR HIGH BUILDING, BUT...
...I DON'T WANT TO ASK FOR YOSHIMORI'S HELP.
MAYBE I SHOULD USE MY SHIKIGAMI TO CARRY OUT THE INVESTIGATION...
RAP
AH!

AAAAAAH!!
YOU'RE YOSHIMORI'S BIG SIS!
HUH?
OH...
...WE MET DURING THE CHERRY BLOSSOM SEASON...
OH.
I'M YURINA KANDA, YOSHIMORI'S CLASSMATE! I DIDN'T KNOW YOU WERE A HIGH SCHOOL STUDENT HERE.
WHAT BRINGS YOU TO THE JUNIOR HIGH SECTION?
WOW
GREAT.
UM...
WELL...
I SEE!
YOU CAME TO SEE YOSHIMORI, RIGHT? DO YOU WANT ME TO GO GET HIM?
HE WASN'T IN THE CLASSROOM JUST A MINUTE AGO, BUT...
OH, NEVER MIND.

OH, THAT'S RIGHT.
NOW I REMEMBER. YOU'RE THE GIRL WITH THE PSYCHIC ABILITY.
DID YOU SEE ANYTHING STRANGE?
OH.
YES.
I DID.
YOU DID?
YES.
I SAW AN OLD MAN BY THE FLOWERBED IN BACK...
AN OLD MAN?
I ALSO SAW A BIG, STRANGE LOOKING, ROUND MAN IN A KIMONO.
THAT MUST BE IT!
WHERE DID YOU SEE HIM?
I'M GLAD YOU ASKED!
I WAS JUST ABOUT TO GO THERE!
GRAB
WHAT?
UM... WELL...
YOU CAN TERMINATE EVIL GHOSTS, CAN'T YOU? JUST LIKE YOSHIMORI?
WHAT?
UH, YES...

BUT YOU KNOW, I'M NOT HIS BIG SISTER...
I'M GLAD YOU CAN.
THIS WAY!
GRAB
PHEW.
I'M AFRAID SHE MISUNDER-STOOD...
YOSHIMORI IS ALMOST LIKE A LITTLE BROTHER TO ME, BUT...
OVER THERE.
I SAW THE MAN IN KIMONO OVER THERE...
WHY ARE YOU HIDING BEHIND THE TREE?
HE LOOKED PRETTY WEIRD WHEN I SAW HIM FROM UPSTAIRS ...
IS THIS...
...MOSS ?
THE MAN IN KIMONO WAS UP THERE WHERE THE MOSS IS, CORRECT?
EEK.
WHOOSH
YES.
IS IT ALL RIGHT TO TOUCH THAT THING?
I THINK SO.
IT'S JUST ORDINARY MOSS.

IF I CHECK OUT OTHER PLACES WHERE THERE IS MOSS...
...I MAY BE ABLE TO TRACK HIM DOWN.
JUNIOR HIGH SCHOOL TEACHERS' OFFICE
EXCUSE ME...
...BUT DID ANYONE SEE THE TEA BISCUITS I KEEP HERE?
OH, MR. KUROSU.
ARE YOU THE ONE WHO ATE THESE SWEETS?
WHAAM
EEK! IS THAT MOLD?!
NO...
THIS IS... MOSS.
IS THIS SOME KIND OF PUNISHMENT?
BY THE WAY, SOMEONE ATE A DOZEN OF MY STRAWBERRY MOCHI SWEETS, TOO.
A DOZEN?

SINCE HIS BIG SIS SAID IT'S GOING TO BE ALL RIGHT...
EVERY-THING SHOULD BE FINE.
RATTLE
BY THE WAY, I FORGOT TO ASK HER NAME.
I REMEMBER YOSHIMORI WAS CALLING HER "TOKI" OR SOME-THING LIKE THAT.
YOSHI-MORI HASN'T COME BACK YET.
I WONDER WHERE HE IS.
...
MUNCH
MUNCH

STARE
ARE THESE... DONUTS?
SHH
FLINCH
HOW DARE YOU!
ZAA
DON'T EVER TOUCH LORD URO!
ZAM
I AM MAMEZO, LORD URO'S AIDE! LISTEN! LORD URO IS SO SUPERIOR THAT A LITTLE BOY LIKE YOU SHOULDN'T...
WAH!
...EVEN DARE TO AP-PROACH HIM!
WOBBLE
AUGH!
AGHRR!!
SMACK

LORD URO! LORD URO! LORD URO!
Oh?
What are you doing in my mouth? Get out of there!
UH, WELL...
...
LISTEN.
SIGH
YOU DON'T SEEM TO BE A BAD GUY SO LET ME GIVE YOU SOME ADVICE.
GET OUT OF HERE IMMEDI-ATELY.
IF YOU DON'T, I WILL HAVE TO TERMINATE YOU.
I'VE WARNED YOU, ALL RIGHT?
I'M GOING TO TAKE A NAP.
The Napping Kekkai: It blocks noises and creates a pleasant environment for sleeping.
ALL RIGHT ...

GASP!
BAM
OH, NO!
I OVERSLEPT!
YOU'RE STILL HERE?
YOU FINALLY WOKE UP, KID!
AH!
ZAM
HOW DID YOU GET THROUGH THE KEKKAI?
LORD URO IS LOOKING FOR A KEKKAISHI!
HUH?

WELCOME, LORD URO!
HERE, PLEASE EAT AS MUCH AS YOU WANT!
THANKS!
NOD
OH, SHUJI. SORRY TO TROUBLE YOU, BUT KEEP THE FOOD COMING.
...ISN'T THIS TOO MUCH FOOD?
I PRE-PARED DINNER AS YOU TOLD ME, BUT...
IS THIS GUY THAT IMPOR-TANT?
WHAT'S THIS? WHY'S MY CROTCHETY OLD GRAND-FATHER BEING SO WELCOM-ING?

!
SHOCK
SHUJI-VISION
SHUJI-VISION
POOF
KLIK
THE FOOD IS BEING EATEN.
OR RATHER, IT'S DISAPPEARING.
GULP
SO...
HE'S HERE FOR SURE!
SHUJI DOESN'T SEE URO SINCE HE DOESN'T HAVE PARA-NORMAL ABILITIES.
OKAY. I'LL COOK SOME MORE!
THANK YOU, SHUJI.
SWISH
BY THE WAY, LORD URO...
...I ASSUME YOU'VE REAPPEARED BECAUSE...
CHOMP

雪村
I COULDN'T FIND HIM.
I WONDER WHO IT WAS.
MOST LIKELY IT WAS LORD URO.
DO YOU KNOW ANYTHING ABOUT HIM, GRANDMA?
LORD URO OVERSEES NATURE.
HE'S SORT OF A DEITY.
HE LAST APPEARED ABOUT 50 YEARS AGO...
I WONDER IF HIS BED BROKE AGAIN.
HIS BED?
ALL THE FOOD IS GONE ALREADY!?
HEY! EVEN MY RICE IS GONE!

I HAVEN'T TOLD YOU THIS YET, BUT LORD URO IS A GUARDIAN DEITY WHO PROTECTS THIS AREA.
HE NORMALLY RESIDES IN THE COLORLESS MARSH NEAR OUR NEIGHBORING TOWN.
Chapter 38: Colorless Marsh
AND HIS BED NEEDS TO BE REPAIRED FROM TIME TO TIME.
SLURP
SLURP
ONE OF OUR FAMILY'S TRADITIONAL DUTIES HAS BEEN TO REPAIR IT.
I REPAIRED IT ONCE 50 YEARS AGO.
YOU DO IT THIS TIME, YOSHIMORI.
ME? WHAT DO YOU ACTUALLY DO TO REPAIR IT?
YOU MUST DO IT VERY CAREFULLY SINCE IT IS A DEITY'S BED.
HOW ABOUT THE YUKIMURAS?
WE DON'T NEED THEIR HELP.
IT'S LATE TONIGHT.
YOU'LL SET OUT TOMORROW. I WILL TELL YOU WHAT YOU NEED TO KNOW BEFORE YOU GO.
MAKE SURE YOU DON'T MAKE CARELESS MISTAKES.
HE'S ALWAYS DECIDING THINGS FOR ME...
AT ANY RATE...

Chapter 38:
Colorless Marsh
WHY ARE YOU HERE? AND WHY ARE YOU WATCHING ME?
I Love Sweets! 100 Recipes

GLANCE
...
THUD
I Love Sweets!
100 Recipes
ALL RIGHT, ALL RIGHT. I'LL MAKE WHATEVER YOU'D LIKE TO EAT. TELL ME WHAT YOU'D LIKE.
Yeah?
Are you sure?
YEAH, I'M SURE.
I ACTUALLY LIKE TO COOK FOR PEOPLE.
ALTHOUGH YOU'RE NOT REALLY A PERSON.

STARE
HMM?
IS THAT WHAT YOU WANT?
DONUTS?
I REMEMBER HE WAS EATING THEM AT LUNCH.
GRB
ALL RIGHT!
I'LL MAKE YOU AS MANY DONUTS AS YOU WANT!
HERE!
EAT UP!
ARE THEY GOOD?
MUNCH
MUNCH

CHOMP
CHOMP
HOW IS IT THAT A DEITY LOVES DONUTS SO MUCH...
DOES IT HAVE SOMETHING TO DO WITH ANGEL'S HALOS? PROBABLY NOT...
OH, LET ME ASK YOU...
YOU'RE A GUARDIAN DEITY OF THIS AREA, RIGHT?
DO YOU KNOW ANYTHING ABOUT THE KARASUMORI SITE, ANYTHING ABOUT ITS MYSTERIOUS POWER?
HEY, KID!
YOU'RE BEING TOO FAMILIAR WITH LORD URO!
OH, IT'S THE LITTLE GUY.
DO YOU WANT SOME, TOO?
I DON'T EAT SUCH FOOD!
DON'T SAY THAT.
SLITHER
YOUR MASTER LOVES THEM.
PONK
PONK
DA
TA
WHAT IS HE DOING?

OH, YOU ATE THEM ALL.
A long, long time ago...
SLURP
SLURP
...there was a deep, dark forest here.
IS HE ANSWERING THE QUESTION ABOUT KARASUMORI?
And I used to live in the middle of that forest.
It was a dark, quiet, and peaceful place.
One day...
...a man appeared.

WOULD YOU PLEASE TURN THIS PLACE OVER TO ME?
I HAVE NEED OF THE POWER OF THIS PLACE.
I said no at first, but...
...since the man prepared a much nicer home for me...
...I gave him the center of the forest.
The forest...
I remember the good old days.
WAIT A MINUTE. ARE YOU TALKING ABOUT LORD KARA-SUMORI?
WHICH FOREST ARE YOU TALKING ABOUT?
Mmm...
HEY!
WAKE UP!
LORD URO IS TIRED. LEAVE HIM ALONE, KID!
Mmm...

WHAT DOES HIS STORY MEAN?
THERE WAS ONCE A DARK, DEEP FOREST HERE.
WAS THAT KARASUMORI FOREST?
WHO IS THE MAN LORD URO SPOKE ABOUT?
GIVEN THE FACT THAT OUR FAMILY REPAIRS LORD URO'S BED...
...IT IS NATURAL TO ASSUME THE MAN IS ONE OF MY ANCESTORS OR MAYBE AN ANCESTOR OF THE YUKIMURAS.
LORD URO DIDN'T REALLY SAY THAT, BUT...
HE'S THINKING AGAIN?
THIS INDEED USED TO BE A FOREST.
I DON'T THINK DEITIES LIE.

HE COULD WELL BE OUR FOUNDING MASTER, TOKIMORI HAZAMA!
IF SO, THE TRADITIONAL STORY THAT HAZAMA WAS HIRED BY LORD KARASUMORI TO TERMINATE AYAKASHI...
...ISN'T ACCURATE.
WELL, IT WOULD MAKE SENSE IF THE KARASUMORI CLAN HAD LIVED SOMEWHERE ELSE...
COULD TOKIMORI HAZAMA POSSIBLY HAVE WORKED FOR THE LORD IN SOME OTHER PLACE?
I HAVE NEED OF THE POWER OF THIS PLACE...
WHY DID HE NEED IT?
AND WHAT DID HE MEAN BY "THE POWER OF THIS PLACE"?
ANYWAY...
...I AM CERTAIN THAT THE STORY I'VE BEEN TOLD CONTAINS SOME INACCURACIES OR LIES.

YOSHI-MORI!
HMM...
TK
TK
DOES LORD URO HAPPEN TO BE AT YOUR HOUSE?
WHAT? YEAH.
DO YOU KNOW ABOUT HIM?
I SEE.
DID HIS BED BREAK AGAIN?
?
YEAH.
GRANDMA TOLD ME...
...SHE HAD BEEN TO HIS PLACE TO REPAIR HIS BED IN THE PAST.
WHAT?
MY GRANDPA TOLD ME HE REPAIRED URO'S BED.
I WONDER IF THEY WENT THERE TOGETHER.
HE TOLD ME WE DIDN'T NEED THE YUKIMURA'S HELP, THOUGH.
SO WHEN ARE YOU GOING TO HIS PLACE?
GRANDMA TOLD ME TO LET YOUR FAMILY TAKE CARE OF IT, BUT...
...I DON'T MIND GOING WITH YOU CAUSE WE ALWAYS DO THESE KINDS OF THINGS TOGETHER.

NO...
YOU DON'T NEED TO.
I NEED MORE ANSWERS FROM LORD URO.
I DON'T WANT TO INVOLVE TOKINE IN ANYTHING DANGEROUS.
IT LOOKS LIKE AN EASY JOB. I CAN HANDLE IT BY MYSELF.
YOU CAN TAKE IT EASY.
BUT I...
DON'T WORRY ABOUT IT.
?
HE'S ACTING STRANGE.
YAWN

WE'RE OFF TO THE COLORLESS MARSH!
HEY, WAIT A MINUTE.
IT'S STILL LIGHT OUTSIDE! WHY ARE YOU DRESSED LIKE THAT?
IDIOT! THIS JOB REQUIRES FORMAL ATTIRE!
AT LEAST LEAVE THE TENKETSU AT HOME!
YOU'LL BE ARRESTED!
QUIET! WHAT ABOUT YOUR SHABBY CLOTHES?
YOU JUST PUT ON A JACKET OVER WHAT YOU WERE ALREADY WEARING, RIGHT?
SHABBY
WHAT?
SWEATS
I CAN'T FORGIVE ANYONE WHO SPEAKS BADLY ABOUT SWEAT PANTS!
GRRRR

YOU BRAT!
HEY, YOU GUYS!
YOU STUBBORN OLD GEEZER!
I CAN'T TAKE IT ANYMORE! I'M GOING TO PUNISH YOU FOR YOUR ROTTEN ATTITUDE!
LET'S GET GOING...
HMPH! I'M GOING TO HIT BACK THEN!
FUME
COME ON, OLD GEEZER! I'LL MAKE YOU APPRECIATE SWEAT PANTS!
ENOUGH! STOP IT, GUYS!
...
SHALL WE GO?
HE CHANGED PANTS.
HE GAVE UP THE TENKETSU AND PUT A JACKET ON OVER HIS KIMONO.
CAN THESE TWO FOOLS REALLY HANDLE THE JOB?
I'LL EXPLAIN WHAT TO DO ALONG THE WAY.
FIRST OF ALL, I WANT YOU TO COMPLETE THE TASK ALL BY YOURSELF.
YEAH.
THAT'S FINE WITH ME.
GOOD. I'LL HAVE THE OPPOR-TUNITY TO ASK LORD URO A LOT OF QUES-TIONS.

THE COLORLESS MARSH
I DON'T SEE ANY TRAIL HERE.
SHUF SHUF
SHUF
SHUF
I'VE BEEN TO THE MARSH SEVERAL TIMES BEFORE, BUT...
...IT LOOKS VERY DIFFERENT FROM BACK HERE.
IT LOOKS VERY DEEP.
MMM.
POING
POING
POING
WE'RE ALMOST THERE.

HIS BED IS AT THE BOTTOM OF THE MARSH, RIGHT?
HOW DO I GET THERE?
JUST WATCH WHAT HE DOES.
INHALE
PUFF
FWOOP

WHIRR
FWP

HEY, WHAT'S THAT BLACK HOLE?
HE MOVED THE WATER FOR YOU.
POING
SWOOSH

HE DISAPPEARED ...
NOW, OFF YOU GO!
I'VE TOLD YOU EVERYTHING YOU NEED TO KNOW.
I'LL BE WAITING HERE.
YOU'D BETTER HURRY UP OR YOU'LL BE LATE FOR YOUR NIGHTLY WORK.
I WONDER IF I'LL...
...HAVE TO KEEP DOING JOBS LIKE THIS?
...LEAPING INTO BLACK HOLES OVER AND OVER AGAIN.
WHAT'S THE MATTER? ARE YOU SCARED?
TK
SEE YOU, GRANDPA!
HERE I GO!

Chapter 39: Divine Field

Chapter 39:
Divine Field

AND WHAT WAS IT THAT I WAS CHASING?

HEY, KID!
?!
NOW I REMEMBER. I'M HERE TO REPAIR LORD URO'S BED.
HEY, KID. HURRY UP AND COME WITH ME!
?
!

My name is ☐ Yoshimori
THIS IS SO UNCOOL...
WHAT ARE YOU DOING, GRANDPA?
YOU ARE ABOUT TO ENTER A DIVINE FIELD.
IF YOU LOSE YOUR CONCENTRATION EVEN FOR A MOMENT, YOU'LL BE SWALLOWED INTO THE FIELD.
THESE ARE YOUR CRIB NOTES.
?
I'LL WRITE WHAT YOU ARE EXPECTED TO DO THERE ON YOUR LEFT HAND.
HEY, HEY.
1. Repair Lord Uro's bed.
2. As soon as I repair the bed, I must come back up to the surface.
YOU DIDN'T NEED TO WRITE THIS. I'LL REMEMBER WHAT TO DO.
IT IS POSSIBLE THAT YOU'LL FORGET.
TO BE MORE PRECISE, YOU MAY GET CONFUSED.

DON'T UNDER-ESTIMATE THE SITUATION YOU'RE ENTERING. IT'S A DANGEROUS PLACE.
IN THE PAST, MANY PEOPLE HAVE FAILED TO RETURN.
THE TASK ITSELF IS VERY SIMPLE.
ALL YOU NEED TO DO IS TO REPAIR THE MAGIC DEVICE LOCATED IN THE CENTER OF HIS BED USING THE KEKKAI TECHNIQUE OF RESTORA-TION.
MAGIC DEVICE?
YOU'LL RECOGNIZE IT ONCE YOU GET THERE.
REMEMBER TO FINISH THE JOB AS QUICKLY AS POSSIBLE.
DON'T STAY THERE TOO LONG.
THE MORE REMIND-ERS YOU HAVE, THE BETTER.
WRITE DOWN ANY-THING YOU DON'T WANT TO FORGET.
DIVINE FIELD, HUH?
Yoshimori
CASTLE CAKES
SEAL OFF THE KARASUMORI SITE
...
KID! HURRY UP!
Y...
YES, SIR!
GASP

IS THIS LORD URO'S BED?
IT LOOKS LIKE A MARIMO ALGAE BALL...
HURRY UP, KID!
TK
HE'S A PAIN IN THE BUTT.
THE ONE WHO WAS HERE LAST TIME WAS MORE ALERT!
HMPH. WAIT AND SEE!
I'LL SHOW YOU THAT I CAN DO A BETTER JOB THAN THAT OLD MAN DID!
SHF
OLD MAN?
OH. GRANDPA WASN'T AN OLD MAN 50 YEARS AGO, WAS HE?
ANYWAY, I'LL DO BETTER THAN THE YOUNG GRANDPA.
SPLASH
SPLASH
IT WAS A WOMAN WHO CAME HERE LAST TIME.

A WOMAN?
YOU MEAN THAT OLD BAG?
NO, SHE WAS A YOUNG WOMAN.
!
BOING BOING
SOUNDS LIKE TOKINE'S GRANDMA.
FWP
FWP
GRANDPA TALKED AS IF HE'D DONE THE JOB ALL BY HIMSELF.
IS THAT WHY HE DIDN'T COME WITH ME?
HOLD ON, TOKIKO. I'LL GO BY MYSELF!

NO, SHIGEMORI!.
YOU'RE TOO INEXPERIENCED FOR THIS JOB.
THAT PLACE IS A DIVINE FIELD, YOU KNOW.
WHAT DID YOU SAY?
DON'T TREAT ME LIKE A BABY!
I AM A LEGITIMATE HEIR JUST LIKE YOU ARE!
BE-SIDES...
...I CAN'T LET A YOUNG GIRL GO TO SUCH A DANGEROUS PLACE ALONE.
DON'T TALK LIKE SUCH A TOUGH GUY...
...UNTIL YOUR KEKKAI TECHNIQUE IS BETTER THAN MINE.
HMPH.
IF MY BIG BROTHER WASN'T SICK IN BED WITH A FEVER...
...I WOULDN'T HAVE NEEDED YOU TO WALK ME HERE.
...

YOU HAVE TO LISTEN TO YOUR ELDERS.
SOMEONE HAS TO STAY UP HERE TO HELP ME RETURN FROM UNDER THE WATER.
I WANT YOU TO DO THAT.
DON'T WORRY.
I'M WELL PREPARED AND I'VE WRITTEN MY NAME ON MY PALM.
OH.
THE WRITING IS PAR-TIALLY GONE...
GIVE ME YOUR HAND.
LET ME REWRITE IT...
...SO YOU'LL BE SURE TO MAKE IT BACK.
...

SHP
SQUISH
...
SHP
GRAB
DARN IT!
PLOPPP

OH.
I DON'T HAVE TO HOLD MY BREATH HERE.
...THIS PLACE FEELS A BIT STRANGE TO ME. IS THIS SOME KIND OF KEKKAI?
IT'S NOT LIKE THE OMINOUS SENSATION I HAD AROUND MY BIG BROTHER, BUT...
IT LOOKS TOO ORDINARY TO BE A DEITY'S BED.
THAT MUST BE THE MAGIC DEVICE.
TK
FWAAP
WOW.
I FEEL WEIGHT-LESS.
SHHH
A BOX?

IT LOOKS OLD...
AM I SUPPOSED TO FIX THE BOX ITSELF OR AM I SUPPOSED TO REPAIR WHAT'S INSIDE?
IT'S EMPTY.
DOES THAT MEAN I SHOULD REPAIR THE BOX?
I SEE IT'S CRACKED.
WHAT AN EASY TASK THIS IS!
LET ME FIX IT RIGHT AWAY SO I CAN ASK LORD URO ABOUT KARASUMORI.
RESTORE!
GLEAM
HUH?
WASN'T I TOLD NOT TO USE THE RESTORATION MAGIC OUTSIDE THE KARASUMORI SITE?

RESTORATION MAGIC USES UP YOUR ENERGY.
A CLEVER JUTSU-SHA WOULD CONSERVE ENERGY BY LETTING HIS SHIKIGAMI DO AS MUCH OF THE WORK AS POSSIBLE.
GRANDPA WAS RIGHT.
I'VE BEEN PUTTING SO MUCH ENERGY INTO FIXING THIS BOX, BUT I HAVEN'T BEEN ABLE TO ACCOMPLISH ANYTHING YET.
I REMEMBER HAVING A HARD TIME TRYING TO REPAIR THINGS AT HOME...
UNNH
DARN IT!
THE KID MUST BE HAVING TROUBLE.
I WONDER IF HE'S ALL RIGHT.
BHAM
?!

RIP
RIP
RIP
ALL RIGHT!
I'VE PUT SO MUCH EFFORT INTO REPAIRING THIS BOX!
NOW IT'S FIXED!
WHAT?
OH!
THE BED HAS GROWN BIGGER!
POING
BOING
HEY.
HOW DO YOU LIKE IT?
PHEW

VRR
RRR
?!
GOOD JOB, KID!
DIZZY
...YOU NOW SHOULD ... HEAD HOME QUICKLY.
RD
HUMANS DON'T HAVE THE MENTAL STRENGTH TO BE ABLE TO SURVIVE HERE FOR VERY LONG.
I'VE GOT IT.
THIS PARTICULAR KEKKAI CAN BE COMPLETE ONLY WHEN A DIVINE PRESENCE INHABITS THE BOX.
IS THIS WHAT'S MEANT BY... "DIVINE FIELD"?

UGH.
I'M BEING SWALLOWED UP!
KID!
PULL YOURSELF TOGETHER! CONCENTRATE ON GETTING HOME!
BRR
HURRY UP.
ONCE LORD URO FALLS ASLEEP, THE HOLE YOU CAME THROUGH WILL BE CLOSED OFF.
NO...
CASTLE CAKES
SEAL OFF THE KARASUMON SITE
NOT YET...
GRB
I HAVE SOME QUESTIONS FOR LORD URO!

I UNDERSTAND...
...THAT I SHOULDN'T STAY HERE ANY MORE.
Chapter 40: Footprints of the Divine
THIS IS THE DIVINE FIELD.
BUT...
CASTLE CAKE
SEAL OFF THE HANASUMON SITE
IT'S SO PERFECT THAT NOTHING CAN...
...PENE-TRATE IT.
I HAVE TO TALK TO LORD URO!

Chapter 40:
Footprints of the Divine

LORD URO!
AH!
BEFORE YOU FALL ASLEEP, PLEASE ANSWER MY QUESTIONS!
SHF
WHICH "FOREST" WERE YOU TELLING ME ABOUT EARLIER? IS IT THE KARASUMORI SITE?
HEY, KID!
IF SO, WHO'S THE LORD OF KARA-SUMORI?
Mmm...
WHO WAS THE MAN THAT YOU SAW AT THE FOREST?
SHAKE SHAKE SHAKE
STOP IT!
ANSWER ME!
WOBBLE
UGH...
GO HOME, KID! HURRY UP!
NO HUMAN CAN STAY HERE FOR TOO LONG!
THE CON-NECTION TO THE UPPER GROUND WILL SOON DISAPPEAR!

I KNOW I'M AN ALIEN PRESENCE HERE.
THE WHOLE PLACE IS REJECTING ME.
CASTLE CAKES
SEAL OFF THE KARASUMORI SITE
I KNOW THAT SO SHUT UP...
AS A KEKKAISHI, I CAN CLEARLY SENSE THAT I SHOULDN'T ...
...STAY HERE ANY LONGER.
BUT...
...AS LONG AS I AM HERE, THIS PLACE CAN'T BE PERFECT...
THAT MEANS YOU WON'T BE FULLY ABLE TO SLEEP.
RIGHT?
SO ANSWER ME!
KID!

STOP BEING UNREASON-ABLE.
YOU SHOULD LEAVE NOW OR YOU'LL BE LOST...
...LIKE THE OTHERS.
I'M SORRY LORD URO, BUT...
...THERE'S SOME-ONE...
YOU SEE...
...SOMEONE I WANT MORE THAN ANYTHING TO PROTECT.
SO I WANT TO KNOW THE ANSWER.
PLEASE ANSWER MY QUES-TIONS...

That man...
...cried when he asked me to give him the forest.
He was sad...
He can't take much more...
FLOP
ZIP
KOI
KOI

WHIRRR
LISTEN, KID!
IT'S COMPLETELY UP TO YOU WHETHER YOU CAN MAKE IT HOME OR NOT NOW!
KEEP FOCUSING ON WHERE YOU BELONG!
BOM
WAS THIS PLACE... SO DARK BEFORE?

WHIRRR
WHAAM
WAH!
AHHHHHHHHH
AH.
THE OPENING IS GETTING SMALLER AND SMALLER...

WHAT?
I, UH...
THAT'S RIGHT. I HAVE TO GO...
GO WHERE?
WHAT? WHERE AM I?
WHERE AM I NOW?
My name is
CASTLE CAKE
SEAL OFF THE
WHAT ARE THESE WRITINGS?
IS IT SUPPOSED TO MEAN SOMETHING TO ME?
I HAVE NO IDEA.
I DON'T UNDERSTAND.
I DON'T UNDERSTAND ANYTHING.

...THERE IS NOTHING HERE.

SOMEBODY, PLEASE...
My name is Yoshimori
CASTLE CAKE
SEAL OFF THE KARASUMORI
...HELP ME!
AAAAAAAH!!
I'M STUCK!
AAAAAAA
MY LEG IS STUCK IN THE TREE!
CREAK
STOP CRYING!
YOU'RE ALL RIGHT.
I'LL HELP YOU WITH ALL MY STRENGTH!
THIS WAY, YOSHI-MORI...

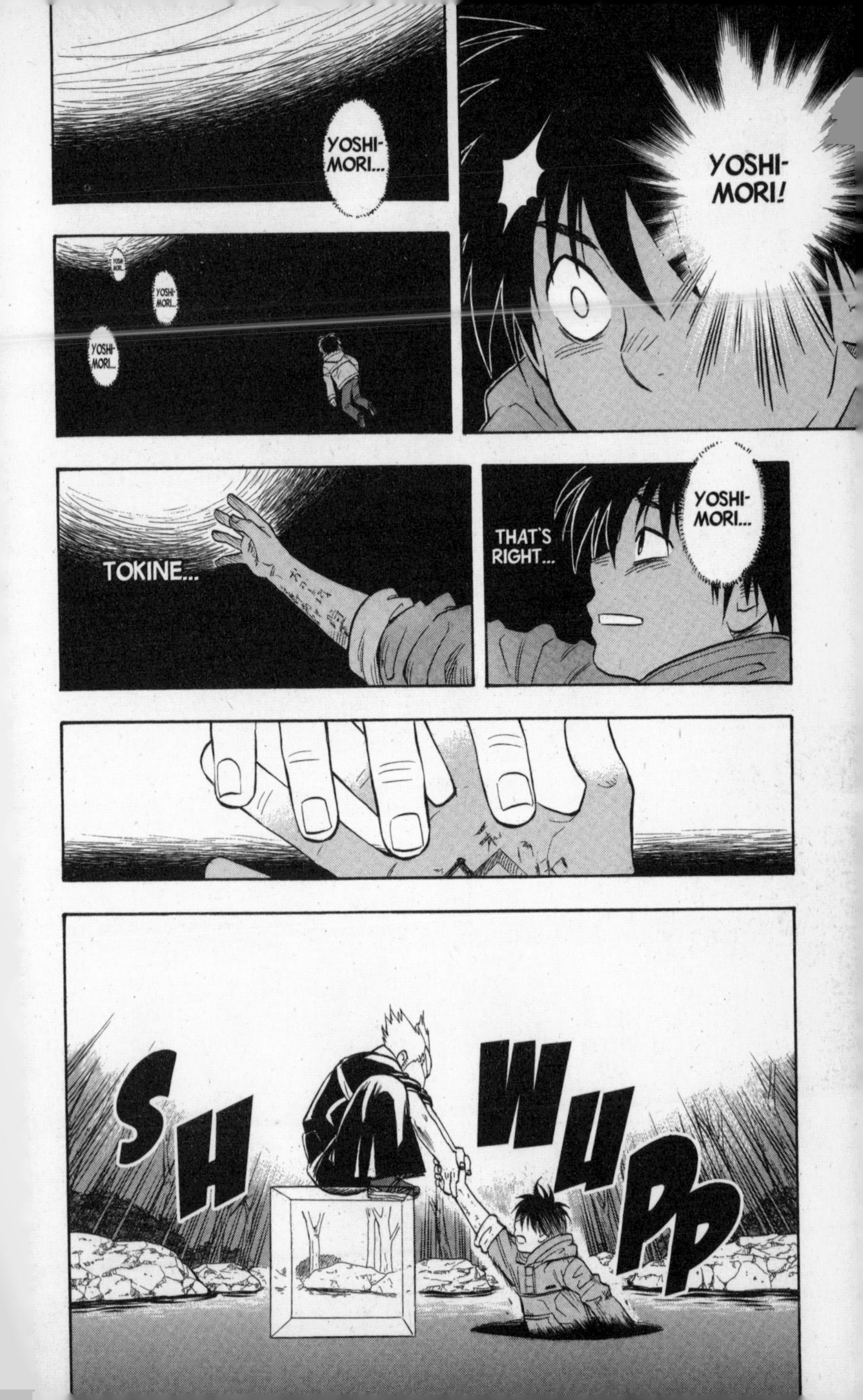

YOSHI-MORI!
YOSHI-MORI...
YOSHI-MORI...
YOSHI-MORI...
YOSHI-MORI...
THAT'S RIGHT...
TOKINE...
SHWUPP

YOSHI-MORI!
AH...
AAAAAAAAA AAAAAAAAAHH!
IT'S ALL RIGHT.
IT'S ALL RIGHT, YOSHI-MORI.
UH...
AAA...
I'M GLAD YOU'RE BACK.
AH...
AAA...
HIC.
SQUEAK SQUEAK
AH?
WHOAAAAA!

HOW COULD I HUG GRANDPA SO TIGHT?
Traumatized
AND I SOBBED WHILE I HELD HIM...
WHY DIDN'T I REALIZE THAT WAS HIM SOONER?
YOSHIMORI.
WANT SOME TEA?
YOU CAME TO YOUR SENSES QUICKLY SO I ASSUME YOU ARE ALL RIGHT, BUT...
NOW I REALLY WANT TO CRY...
I'M SORRY I GAVE YOU SUCH A DIFFICULT JOB.
MAYBE I SHOULD HAVE REPAIRED THE BED.
I SENT YOU THERE...
...BECAUSE I SOMEHOW FELT I SHOULD.
UNLIKE ME...
...YOU STILL HAVE PLENTY OF ROOM TO GROW.
ALSO ...
...STRANGE THINGS HAVE BEEN HAPPENING THESE DAYS.
THE REPAIRS TO LORD URO'S BED, FOR EXAMPLE ...
..WOULD NORMALLY LAST FOR 100 YEARS.
THAT'S WHY I WASN'T PREPARED TO TELL YOU ABOUT LORD URO YET.

HEY, GRANDPA. I DON'T REALLY UNDER-STAND.
FIRST OF ALL, THE STORY ABOUT WHAT HAPPENED 50 YEARS AGO...
WELL, WHAT WAS THAT KEKKAI ANYWAY?
YOSHIMORI... YOU'RE STILL CONFUSED, AREN'T YOU?
I DON'T UNDERSTAND WHAT YOU ARE TALKING ABOUT.
DARN IT! MY HEAD IS SPINNING.
WHY DON'T YOU REST FOR A WHILE?
YOU ARE NOT CAPABLE OF UNDER-STANDING ANYTHING RIGHT NOW.
THERE ARE...
...MANY THINGS I HAVEN'T TOLD YOU YET.
CALM DOWN.
CALM DOWN.
WHAT IS ONE PLUS ONE?
YOSHI-MORI... DO YOU WANT ME TO SUBSTITUTE FOR YOU TONIGHT?
SHUT UP! I'M FINE!
HOW DID IT GO?

WERE YOU ABLE TO REPAIR LORD URO'S BED?
YEAH.
MY GRANDMA DIDN'T EXPLAIN MUCH ABOUT IT...
CAN YOU TELL ME WHAT IT WAS LIKE?
NO WORDS CAN... EXPLAIN THAT PLACE.
HEY!
THERE WAS NOTHING SPECIAL ABOUT IT.
IN A NUTSHELL, IT'S LIKE A MARIMO ALGAE BALL.
ALGAE BALL?
LET ME ASK YOU THIS THEN.
WHY HAVE YOU BEEN AVOIDING LOOKING AT ME?
GASP
I DON'T KNOW WHY, BUT?
...
...IT FELT AS IF TOKINE HAD RESCUED ME EVEN THOUGH SHE WASN'T THERE...
YOSHI-MORI!
WAIT UP!
YOSHI-MORI!
SHUT UP! STOP SCREAMING MY NAME!

YOSHI-MORI.
YOSHI-MORI!
C'MON, WAKE UP!
WE HAVE A PROBLEM.
SHAK!
SHAK!
GRMBL...
I CLEANED UP THE MOSS THAT WAS ALL OVER THE HOUSE AFTER LORD URO LEFT, BUT...
LOOK...
ZA—ZAM
THERE'S A TREE IN THE KITCHEN.
THIS IS WHERE LORD URO WAS SITTING...
WHAT SHOULD WE DO?
AND THE TREE BORE SOME KIND OF FRUIT...
ARE THESE... DONUTS?!
WOW...

I WISH I HAD CHECKED INSIDE THE SCHOOL LAST NIGHT...
Y-YOSHIMORI, WHAT IS ALL THIS?
SOME KIND OF PLANT CURSE?
OH, DON'T WORRY. I DON'T THINK IT'S HARMFUL.
HMM?
I WONDER...
WOW!
RUSTLE
NOW I HAVE A BED OF GRASS.
OH WELL.
GUESS I CAN TAKE A NAP BEFORE I CLEAN UP THIS MESS.
TEACHERS' OFFICE
...
THERE'S A GIANT STRAWBERRY ON MR. KUROSU'S DESK!

Chapter 41:
Toshi-
Mori's
Days
YAWN
Wonder Dog

HEY, TOSHI.
HEE
ARE YOU...
HEE
...FREE TODAY?
YO!
HEE
TOSHIMORI'S CLASSMATE TAICHI KOMAGOME. HIS NICKNAME IS KONTA.
TOSHIMORI'S CLASSMATE GAKU MIKAWAJIMA. HIS NICKNAME IS GATCHO.
...
YOU WANT ME TO HELP YOU WITH YOUR SPECIAL ASSIGN-MENT, DON'T YOU?
YOU'RE SUPPOSED TO DO YOUR OWN HOMEWORK.
CLASS OFFICER
YOU WON'T LEARN ANYTHING IF YOU DON'T DO IT YOURSELF.
WE DON'T NEED A LECTURE FROM YOU!

I'VE TOLD YOU THIS MANY TIMES...
AS LONG AS YOU DO YOUR HOME-WORK, IT DOESN'T MATTER IF SOME OF YOUR ANSWERS ARE WRONG. AS LONG AS YOU TURN SOMETHING IN, THE TEACHER WILL STOP GIVING YOU OUT THESE SPECIAL ASSIGN-MENTS TO PUNISH YOU. UNDERSTAND?
...WHAT'S IN IT FOR ME?
LISTEN, TOSHI. NOBODY'S PERFECT, ALL RIGHT?
WHY DON'T YOU JUST HELP US?
BUT...
WOW. YOU LOOK LIKE AN ANGEL, BUT YOU TALK LIKE A DEVIL.
COME ON...
DOESN'T FRIEND-SHIP MEAN ANYTHING TO YOU?
HOW ABOUT THIS...
JUST GIVE US ADVICE ON HOW TO SOLVE THE PROBLEMS. WE'LL DO THE REST.
THAT WAY WE CAN LEARN AND...
...IT WILL BE GOOD FOR YOU SINCE YOU CAN LEARN MORE BY TEACHING US.
YEAH!
AND OUR FRIENDSHIP WILL GROW STRONGER. EVERYONE WILL BE HAPPY, RIGHT?
I THINK ...
...THIS STILL WORKS MORE TO YOUR ADVANTAGE.
PLEASE JUST HELP US!
OM
HMM ...
NONE OF THE OTHER SMART STUDENTS IN THE CLASS CAN HELP US BECAUSE THEY ALL HAVE CRAM SCHOOLS TO GO TO.
YOU'RE THE ONLY ONE WE CAN ASK FOR HELP!
ZO
ALL RIGHT, ALL RIGHT...
WAHOO !

DING DONG DING DONG
WHAT?
YOU WANT TO COME TO MY HOUSE?
WHY CAN'T WE GO TO KONTA'S LIKE USUAL?
'CAUSE YOUR PARENTS AREN'T HOME.
MY DAD TOOK A DAY OFF TODAY AND HE'S AT HOME SLEEPING.
HOW ABOUT YOUR HOUSE, GATCHO?
MY PLACE IS SMALL AND MY BROTHERS WILL GET IN OUR WAY.
BESIDES, WE'RE KIND OF CURIOUS ABOUT YOUR HOUSE.
I WANT TO SEE THAT DOG, MASURAO, YOU'RE ALWAYS BRAGGING ABOUT.
MADARAO ISN'T VERY FRIENDLY TO STRANGERS.
GRANDPA AND DAD ARE BOTH OUT TODAY.
THESE TWO MIGHT GET OUT OF HAND IF THEY FIND THAT OUT...
C'MON! LET'S GO TO YOUR HOUSE!
WELL...
LET ME WARN YOU...

...MY BIG BROTHER IS A VERY SCARY GUY.
CAN YOU PROMISE YOU'LL BEHAVE YOURSELVES?
UH... SURE...
THAT SHOULD DO IT...
I'VE NEVER BEEN IN THIS NEIGHBORHOOD.
THESE HOUSES ARE ALL HUGE.
DO YOU THINK TOSHIMORI'S FAMILY IS RICH?
I DUNNO.
HEY!
TOKINE!
HEY, TOSHIMORI. COMING HOME FROM SCHOOL?
TK TK
YEAH!

IS THIS YOUR SISTER, TOSHIO?
NOPE.
ARE THESE YOUR FRIENDS?
YOU GUYS...
GIGGLE
...ALWAYS BUY SNACKS ON THE WAY HOME?
BLUSH
SHE'S PRETTY...
OH.
HEY, TOSHIMORI.
DO YOU THINK...
...YOSHIMORI'S BEEN ACTING STRANGE LATELY?
WHAT?
HAS HE?
YOSHIMORI ALWAYS ACTS STRANGE...
SINCE HE REPAIRED LORD URO'S BED...NO, SINCE YOUR BROTHER, MASAMORI, CAME BACK FOR THAT VISIT...
HE'S BEEN ACTING WEIRD.
MAYBE TOSHIMORI'S TOO YOUNG TO NOTICE.
WELL, NEVER MIND.
FORGET ABOUT IT, OKAY?

BYEBYE
SEE YOU.
WHAT A HUGE HOUSE!
SHE'S NICE.
AND SHE LIVES IN A HUGE HOUSE.
HM?
HEY!
YOU LIVE NEXT DOOR TO HER?
YEAH.
IS SHE RICH?
WOW!
HEY, THE DOG ISN'T HERE!
GRAB
COME OUT, DOGGY!
MAD!
DURING THE DAY, MADARAO IS...
THERE'S A WARE-HOUSE!
A WARE-HOUSE!
LET'S GO LOOK FOR TREA-SURES!
DK
HEY, DON'T FORGET WHY WE'RE HERE!
GRRR
YOU BETTER BEHAVE YOUR-SELVES.
OR MY BIG BROTHER WILL BE VERY ANGRY!

TAA
DA
HEY, TOSHIMORI.
WHEN'D YOU GET HOME?
DID YOUR FRIENDS COME OVER TO PLAY?
WEL-COME.
SLUMP
HEY, DO YOU KNOW WHY GRANDPA AND DAD AREN'T HOME?
DID YOU FORGET? DAD IS IN TOKYO FOR A MEETING ABOUT HIS NEW NOVEL...
...AND GRANDPA IS OUT WITH HIS SENIORS CLUB AND WON'T BE HOME UNTIL LATE.
OH, IS THAT SO?
THEY TOLD US ABOUT IT LAST NIGHT, REMEMBER?
HE'S THE SCARY BROTHER?
HMM.

WHAT ABOUT DINNER?
DAD LEFT A NOTE ABOUT IT.
YOSHIMORI.
WE'RE GOING TO STUDY HERE SO DON'T GET IN OUR WAY, OKAY?
OKAY...
EXCUSE US.
YOUR BROTHER ISN'T SCARY AT ALL.
HE LOOKED LIKE AN ORDINARY GUY.
BUT WHY IS HE DRESSED LIKE SOMEBODY'S MOTHER?
DARN IT! YOSHIMORI RUINED MY PLAN.
HEY, IS YOUR DAD A NOVELIST?
LET'S JUST START WORKING ON YOUR HOMEWORK.
TOSHIMORI LOOKED KIND OF MAD...
THIS MUST BE THE NOTE.
FLAP
Yoshimori,
Since grandpa is also coming home late, I asked Mrs. Yukimura to fix you a dinner. Dad
Tokine may be delivering the meal to you!
父

TOKINE'S BRINGING DINNER FOR US?
BLUSH
HERE'S YOUR ORDER!
HIGHLY UNLIKELY
BUT HER MOTHER MIGHT BRING THE FOOD.
HIGHLY UNLIKELY
HEY, GUYS!
LET ME EXPLAIN ...
TA DA
I BROUGHT YOU SOMETHING TO EAT!

WOW! DID YOU MAKE THIS?
HEY, CAN WE EAT IT ALL? IS IT OKAY TO EAT IT ALL?
HAHAHA
SURE. EAT AS MUCH AS YOU WANT!
WHY IS HE IN SUCH A GOOD MOOD?
HEY, YOSHIMORI. WE'RE TRYING TO STUDY...
WOW! THIS IS SO GOOD!
MUNCH MUNCH
CAN'T EAT ANOTHER BITE.
HUMPH
YOU REALLY RUINED THINGS, YOSHIMORI.
HOW CAN A GUY LIKE HIM BE OUR FAMILY'S LEGITIMATE HEIR?
HEY, WE HAVEN'T MADE ANY PROGRESS!
CAN I TAKE THE LEFTOVERS HOME FOR MY BROTHERS?
IT MUST BE GREAT TO HAVE A BROTHER WHO CAN MAKE STUFF LIKE THIS.
BOUF
PLUS, YOU LIVE IN SUCH A BIG HOUSE.
THAT'S RIGHT. YOUR HOUSE IS SO HUGE.

YAHOO!
TIME TO GO EXPLORE!
WHAT?!
DK
I WANT TO SEE THE WARE-HOUSE!
C'MON, TOSHI!
WAIT!
DK DK DK
HOW HUGE!
HOW MANY ROOMS ARE THERE?
WOW. THERE'S A POND IN THE GARDEN!
IS THIS SCROLL VERY VALUABLE?
HEY, DO YOU HAVE ANY SECRET ROOMS IN THE HOUSE?
HOW ABOUT AN ATTIC?
PANIC
PANIC
NO...
DON'T DO THAT.
I STILL WANT TO SEE THE WARE-HOUSE!
STOP IT!
CHA

YOSHI-MORI...
WHAT...
WHAT SHOULD I DO?
I THOUGHT THEY MIGHT WRECK THE HOUSE...
...SO I USED A KEKKAI TECH-NIQUE TO STOP THEM...
AND THEN...
THEY BUMPED INTO EACH OTHER REAL HARD...
PONK

DON'T WORRY.
THEY JUST FAINTED.
THEY'LL BE FINE IN A LITTLE WHILE.
I CAN'T BELIEVE I USED KEKKAI ON MY FRIENDS...
I'VE ZAPPED MY FRIENDS MANY TIMES.
HOWEVER, YOU MAY NEED TO IMPROVE YOUR SKILLS A BIT MORE.
TOKINE.
雪村
YES?
WILL YOU DELIVER THIS TO THE NEIGHBORS FOR ME?
HUH?
BOTH SHUJI AND HIS FATHER-IN-LAW ARE AWAY THIS EVENING.
THERE'S CURRY IN THE POT.
SERVE THE RICE AND CURRY FOR THEM WHEN YOU GET THERE, WILL YOU?

HELLO?
IS ANYONE HOME...?
OH, THE DOOR'S OPEN.
EXCUSE ME.
HOW CARELESS...
HEY, YOSHIMORI...
RUSTLE
MMM?
SHK
OH, THEY'RE UP.
I... I'M SORRY...
YOU'D BETTER COOL YOUR HEAD A LITTLE WHILE LONGER.
TOSHIMORI TOLD ME YOU FELL PRETTY HARD.
RIGHT?

WE FELL?
I DUNNO.
DOES IT HURT ANYWHERE BESIDES YOUR FOREHEADS?
EEEEE!
THAT VOICE!
DK
DK
WHAT'S GOING ON?
SL
TOKINE, ARE YOU OKAY?
NOOOO
THIS IS EXACTLY THE KIND OF MOMENT WHEN I WISH I COULD USE KEKKAI EFFECTIVELY, BUT...
...I'M NOT SKILLFUL ENOUGH YET.

IT SEEMED YOSHIMORI WAS TOO PREOCCUPIED WITH SOMETHING TO USE KEKKAI TO STOP THE DISASTER...
AS A RESULT, WE GOT CURRY ALL OVER OURSELVES.
SPLOOOSH
I'M...
I'M SO SORRY...
...
AND I...
MY HAIR STILL SMELLS LIKE CURRY.
I'M SORRY ...
DON'T WORRY ABOUT IT.
WELL, HOW ABOUT GIVING US THE ANSWERS TO OUR SPECIAL ASSIGNMENT TO MAKE UP FOR IT?
...ENDED UP DOING SOMETHING WHICH WASN'T GOOD FOR MY FRIENDS (IN THE LONG RUN).

I'M REALLY SORRY ABOUT TODAY.
NO, WE HAD A GOOD TIME.
YOUR BROTHER IS FUN, TOO.
MY OLDEST BROTHER IS COOLER, BUT...
WHAT? I LIKE YOUR BROTHER.
PLUS, HE'S A GREAT BAKER.
WELL...
I GUESS SOMETIMES HE IS A GOOD BIG BROTHER TO ME.
WE HAD DINNER DELIVERED THAT NIGHT.
YOSHIMORI SEEMED A BIT DEPRESSED, BUT...
WHY COULDN'T I HAVE WARDED OFF THE CURRY? TO MAKE THINGS WORSE, TOKINE AND I FEEL MORE AWKWARD AROUND EACH OTHER NOW.
SIGH
...SINCE HE'S SUCH A SIMPLE GUY, IT DIDN'T TAKE VERY LONG FOR HIM TO GET OVER IT.
HEY! THIS PORK CUTLET BOWL TASTES GREAT!
YUM!

Chapter 42: Secrets

CHA
KETSU!
WHAM

ALL RIGHT!
NOW I KNOW HOW TO CREATE MULTI-LAYERED KEKKAI.
THIS WAY I CAN COMPEN-SATE FOR THE STRENGTH OF MY KEKKAI.
BUT...
MY STAMINA HAS ITS LIMITS.
I CAN'T USE THIS TECHNIQUE THAT MANY TIMES IN ONE DAY.
THAT'S...
...NOT A GOOD TECHNIQUE FOR YOU.

I'LL SEE YOU LATER.
雪村
HMM...
WHAT SORT OF TECH-NIQUE IS GOOD FOR ME THEN?
SIGH
YOSHI-MORI...
IT'S UNUSUAL THAT HE'S LEAVING FOR SCHOOL BEFORE I DO.
HE'S BEEN ACTING STRANGE LATELY.
HE'S ALWAYS THINKING ABOUT SOMETHING AND I THINK HE'S AVOIDING ME.
MORE THAN ANYTHING, THOUGH...
HE'S HIDING SOMETHING FROM ME...
I JUST KNOW IT.

MAYBE HE'S DOING SOME SPECIAL TRAINING IN SECRET.
A NEW TECH-NIQUE?
...
WHAT AM I DOING?
I'LL JUST ASK HIM ABOUT IT DIRECTLY.
YOSHI-MORI!
HMM?
SLURRRP
HEY, TOKINE!
OH, DID THIS SHOCK YOU?
FOR THE LAST COUPLE DAYS I FORGOT TO DRINK MY COFFEE-FLAVORED MILKS.
SO I'M DRINKING THREE OF THEM AT ONCE TODAY.
COFFEE MILK

YOU MAY NOT...
...KNOW THIS, BUT...
...WE GET COFFEE-FLAVORED MILK AT LUNCH TODAY, TOO!
TP TP TP TP TP TP TP TP
HEY, WAIT!
WHAT A DORK!
HEY, YOU'RE THE ONE THAT WANTED TO TALK TO ME!
I FEEL STUPID...
...FOR EVEN THINKING THAT HE WAS BEING SERIOUS ABOUT SOME-THING.
THE KARASUMORI SITE USED TO BE A FOREST IN WHICH DEITIES RESIDED, AND TOKIMORI HAZAMA SHOWED UP THERE ONE DAY.
I JUST DON'T GET IT...
DOES THAT TELL ME ANY-THING?

HOW CAN I FIND THE TRUTH ABOUT THE SITE?
SHK
ISN'T THIS...?
GRAND-PA!
DK DK DK DK DK DK
SLAM
I HAVE A QUESTION FOR YOU.

ABOUT KEKKAI?
YEAH. IT SAYS HERE...
...THAT THE FARTHER A KEKKAISHI STEPS AWAY FROM A KEKKAI HE'S CREATED, THE LESS EFFECTIVE THE KEKKAI WILL BE.
THAT MEANS EXTRA FORCE IS NEEDED TO LOCK IN A KEKKAI IF A KEKKAISHI CAN'T STAY AT THE SPOT WHERE IT'S CREATED.
TAKE FOR EXAMPLE, THE MAGIC DEVICE AT LORD URO'S BED.
IT MUST TAKE QUITE A BIT OF POWER TO SURROUND A DEITY.
OVER TIME, ITS POWER WANES, AND A KEKKAISHI MUST GO THERE TO RECHARGE IT.
AM I RIGHT?
WELL, YES YOU ARE, BUT...
...WHAT ARE YOU GOING TO DO WITH THIS KNOWLEDGE?

NOTHING IN PARTICULAR.
BESIDES, WHAT'S WRONG WITH A KEKKAISHI WANTING TO FIND OUT MORE ABOUT KEKKAI?
IT MAKES SENSE...
...THAT ONE WOULD NEED SOMETHING VERY POWERFUL TO CONTAIN A VERY POWERFUL THING.
IT MEANS THAT A VERY POWERFUL FORCE WOULD BE REQUIRED TO SEAL OFF THE WHOLE KARASUMORI SITE.
I WONDER IF TOKIMORI HAZAMA WANTED TO USE THE POWER OF LORD URO'S LAND TO SEAL OFF KARASUMORI?
WHATEVER HAPPENED, IT HASN'T COMPLETELY SEALED OFF THE KARASUMORI SITE...
HMM.
WILL I EVER BE ABLE TO FIX IT?
THERE MUST BE A WAY TO DO IT.
BUT IT SEEMED LIKE THE KEKKAI CREATED AT LORD URO'S BED WAS DIFFERENT FROM THE ONES WE NORMALLY USE.
NOT THE SHAPE OF IT, BUT MAYBE IT HAD SOME KIND OF DIFFERENT QUALITY. I WONDER SPECIFICALLY HOW IT'S DIFFERENT?

YOSHI-MORI.
DON'T TRY TO UNDER-STAND EVERY-THING SO QUICKLY.
I SENT YOU THERE BECAUSE THAT WAS A VERY RARE OPPORTUNITY, BUT...
...DO NOT THINK ABOUT IT TOO MUCH. JUST REMEMBER HOW IT FELT.
YOU SHOULDN'T STICK YOUR NOSE TOO FAR INTO THIS MATTER UNTIL YOU FULLY MASTER THE HAZAMA-RYU TECHNIQUES.
?
THE KEKKAI CREATED AT LORD URO'S BED ISN'T HAZAMA-RYU?
I THOUGHT TOKIMORI HAZAMA MADE THE GOD'S BED.
THE KEKKAI AT LORD URO'S BED IS DIFFER-ENT.
HAZAMA-RYU KEKKAI IS THE METHOD MASTER TOKIMORI HAZAMA INVENTED. HE DEVELOPED IT IN SUCH A WAY THAT IT WOULD BE EASY FOR KEKKAISHI TO LEARN.
ANYHOW, WHAT YOU NEED TO DO NOW IS TO CONCENTRATE ON YOUR CURRENT TRAINING.
JUST FOCUS ON LEARNING HOW TO USE YOUR ABILITIES PROPERLY.

SHF
POWER WITHOUT THE PROPER TRAINING TO USE IT...
...CAN ONLY RESULT IN DOING HARM.
YOSHI-MORI.
I'VE MENTIONED THIS BEFORE, BUT...
...STRANGE THINGS HAVE BEEN HAPPENING AT THE KARASUMORI SITE.

BE CAREFUL.

WHY DON'T YOU STOP THINKING ABOUT IT?
I KNOW PEOPLE TEND TO WORRY ABOUT THINGS WHEN THEY ARE YOUNG, BUT...
...YOUR STRONG POINT IS YOUR ABILITY TO ACT WITHOUT HESITATION. AM I WRONG?
HUMPH.
THIS IS NO FUN FOR ME AT ALL
HEY, MADA-RAO.

WHAT WAS TOKIMORI HAZAMA LIKE?
WHAT?
WHAT WAS HE LIKE?
HE WAS SUCH A GOOD-LOOKING MAN.
GUSH
HE WAS SLIM AND HAD A GENTLE DEMEANOR. AND HE WAS QUITE ELEGANT.
YET WHEN HE NEEDED TO BE, HE WAS VERY MANLY...
GUSH
GUSH
THAT'S NOT WHAT I WANT TO KNOW...
HIS EYES WERE SOMETHING...
OH, BUT THE BEST THING ABOUT HIM WAS HIS VOICE.
HE HAD KIND OF A LOW VOICE THAT GETS UNDER YOUR SKIN...
PHEW
WELL, THAT'S NOT WHAT I...
IMAGINE SUCH A VOICE CALLING YOUR NAME!
YOU'D DO JUST ABOUT ANYTHING HE ASKS OF YOU!
LISTEN TO ME!
KYA AA
SO...
TELL ME...
HOW HE...
...USED HIS KEKKAI TECHNIQUES.

HE CREATED KEKKAI THE SAME WAY YOU GUYS DO...
THAT'S NOT WHAT I MEAN...
WELL ...
LET ME SEE IF I CAN DEMON-STRATE.
SHWM
THIS IS WHAT I MEAN...
HMM...
HUMPH...! UGH...
UGH!
?
WHAT ARE YOU STRAIN-ING YOUR-SELF FOR?
GAAAA!
I DON'T KNOW HOW TO DO IT, DARN IT!
I NEED TO CALM DOWN AND TRY TO REMEMBER HOW I FELT WHEN I WAS AT URO'S PLACE.
MAYBE MADARAO WILL UNDERSTAND BETTER IF I SHOW HIM THE TECHNIQUE MASAMORI USED.
OH.
YOSHI-MO--

RUMBLE
RUMBLE
RUMBLE
WHAT?

YOSHI-MORI!
GASP!
DON'T STARTLE ME LIKE THAT!
TP TP TP TP TP
WHAT WERE YOU TRYING TO DO JUST NOW?
WHAT?
I WASN'T DOING ...
...ANY-THING SPECIAL ...
I DIDN'T QUITE UNDER-STAND, BUT...
...IT FELT LIKE YOU WERE TRYING TO DO SOME-THING DANGER-OUS.
AM I WRONG?

WHAT DO YOU MEAN BY SOME-THING DANGER-OUS?
I CAN'T TELL WHAT IT WAS EXACTLY, BUT I FELT THAT YOU WERE DOING SOMETHING DANGEROUS.
GRB
LET ME TELL YOU. AS SOON AS MY BACK IS TURNED, YOU'RE ALWAYS UP TO SOMETHING!
SWP
AH!
SHUT UP!
STOP TREATING ME LIKE A LITTLE KID!
I'M THE KIND OF GUY WHO ISN'T INTIMIDATED BY ANY CHALLENGE!
HEY, WAIT!
ZM ZM ZM
HUMPH!
WHAT AN IRRITATING KID HE IS!
WHAT AN ATTITUDE!
IS HE GOING THROUGH A REBEL-LIOUS STAGE?
A LATE BLOOMER?

THAT'S KARA-SUMORI.
CUR-RENTLY, A SCHOOL IS BUILT ON THE SITE.
AS I EXPLAINED TO YOU EARLIER...
...YOU'LL BE ABLE TO OBTAIN AS MUCH POWER AS YOU WISH IF YOU CAN MANAGE TO STAY THERE LONG ENOUGH.
FWAA
WHIRR
WHIRR
WHIRR
WHIRR

FWAAA
WE ARE ALLOWED TO DO WHATEVER WE WANT?
YES, YOU ARE.
AS LONG AS YOU STICK WITHIN THE GUIDELINES I'VE LAID OUT FOR YOU.

Chapter 43: Feathers
LET'S GO OVER IT AGAIN.
YOU ARE GOING TO ENTER SIMULTANEOUSLY FROM THE SKY, GROUND AND AIR IN ORDER TO CONFUSE THEM.
BUT DON'T GO TOO DEEP BENEATH THE GROUND.
AFTER BREAKING INTO THE SITE, YOU ARE GOING TO HIDE AT YOUR SPECIFIED POSITIONS FOR A WHILE.
SHOULD A KEKKAISHI FIND YOU, KEEP RUNNING AWAY FROM HIM WITHIN YOUR ASSIGNED AREA. DON'T FIGHT BACK.
WHEN THE TIME COMES, I'LL GIVE YOU THE GO-AHEAD. AFTER THAT, YOU ARE FREE TO DO WHATEVER YOU LIKE.
SOUNDS LIKE A STUPID PLAN.
DON'T SAY THAT. THE PLAN IS BASED ON A LOT OF RESEARCH AND...
THAT'S REALLY STUPID.
HUMPH...
YOU GUYS DON'T WANT TO BE PUNISHED FOR NOT FOLLOWING ORDERS, DO YOU?

GO NOW.
Chapter 43:
Feathers

SO TELL ME.
TELL YOU WHAT?
IT'S NONE OF YOUR BUSINESS.
TUP
TUP
WELL.
I CAN GUESS WELL ENOUGH ON MY OWN.
WHAT ARE YOU PLANNING TO DO?
YOU WANT TO KNOW MORE ABOUT THE KARASUMORI SITE.
YOUR QUESTIONS ABOUT MASTER HAZAMA AND KEKKAI ARE ALL RELATED TO THAT, AREN'T THEY?
AND YOU WANT TO KEEP TOKINE AWAY FROM YOUR INVESTIGATION BECAUSE YOU'RE WORRIED SHE COULD GET HURT.
YOU MUST BE THINKING OF SEALING OFF THE KARASUMORI SITE, AM I RIGHT?
GASP

WHAA AA
WHAT A STUPID BOY YOU ARE!
HEH HEH HEH HEH
EVEN MASTER HAZAMA COULDN'T DO IT.
AND YOU THINK YOU CAN?
I'LL...
I'LL NEVER KNOW UNLESS I TRY!
HA HA HA HA!
WHAT ?!
YOU'RE RIGHT.
A SMART GUY WOULDN'T HAVE TO TRY TO KNOW THAT'S IMPOSSIBLE.
HEE HEE
...
HUMPH. SAY WHATEVER YOU WANT.
I AM GOING TO DO IT.
WHOOOOSH
HEE HEE
I'M NOT GOING TO STOP YOU FROM TRYING.

PEOPLE AROUND YOU MAY OPPOSE THIS IDEA OF YOURS, BUT...
...I BELIEVE A LITTLE RECKLESSNESS REALLY SUITS YOU.
MADARAO, DON'T TELL TOKINE ABOUT THIS, OKAY?
ALL RIGHT.
SHE SEEMS TO BE IN A BAD MOOD...
I WONDER WHAT YOSHIMORI IS UP TO.
I REMEMBER GETTING THAT SAME FEELING ONCE IN THE PAST.
I HAD...
...A BAD FEELING JUST LIKE THIS.

NOT ONLY THAT, I FEEL FRUS- TRATED.
I WON- DER WHY.
SHEEEEN
OH.
I GUESS A FEW AYAKASHIS HAVE APPEARED.
THERE ARE THREE.
LET'S GO, HAKUBI.
IT'S STRANGE.
I DETECT THE SAME AYAKASHI SCENT FROM SEVERAL DIFFERENT DIREC- TIONS.
WHAT'S STRANGE ?
DID YOU FIND THEM YET, MADA- RAO?
WHAT DOES THAT MEAN?

FWASH
AH!
FWO
OP
YOSHIMORI! THERE'S MORE THAN ONE AYAKASHI HERE. FINISH THAT ONE OFF QUICKLY!
I KNOW THAT!
DAA
ASH
I'M GOING TO GET YOU...
CHA

KETSU!
WHAM
WSSSH
FWOOP
UGH...
WHAT A MISERABLE PERFORM-ANCE.
YOU DIDN'T EVEN TOUCH IT WITH THAT HUGE KEKKAI.
SHUT UP!
AS LONG AS IT REMAINS WITHIN A SHORT DISTANCE, I CAN ELIMINATE IT!
ZK
ZK
ZK
ZK

DK
DK
SHKK
DK
DK
SMIRK

SHF
WHI
IRR
?!
UGH!
IS IT GOING TO ATTACK ME...?!
I'VE BEEN EN-CLOSED!
PI
NG
THUK

SHF
WHIRR
IT RAN AWAY?!
THERE IT IS!
FWOOP
SH
WHAT?
HONEY!
ANOTHER INTRUDER.
THIS ODOR IS...THAT OF A HUMAN.
WAIT!
DK
DK

I SEE.
THAT BOY CAN FIGHT AN AERIAL BATTLE BY PITCHING SEVERAL KEKKAI IN THE AIR AND THEN JUMPING FROM ONE KEKKAI TO ANOTHER, EH?
I GUESS I SHOULD REPORT THIS TO MY PEOPLE.
THE ACCURACY OF HIS KEKKAI SEEMS TO DETERIORATE WHEN HE PITCHES IT A LONG DISTANCE, BUT...
...IN THEORY, AS LONG AS HE CAN LOCATE THE TARGET CORRECTLY, HE CAN CAPTURE IT IN HIS KEKKAI. THIS TECHNIQUE COULD BE MORE EFFECTIVE THAN I WAS LED TO BELIEVE.
KETSU!
WHAAMM
SHOO

WHIRR
ZZZIP
AH!
WHIRR
UGH...
THAT AYAKASHI CAN DIS-ASSEMBLE ITS BODY INTO SMALL PARTS...
MY KEKKAI ISN'T STRONG ENOUGH TO WITHSTAND SUCH A FOCUSED AYAKASHI THRUST?
FWOOOP
DARN IT.
THIS IS A PAIN IN THE NECK!
CHA
WHAM
I'LL JUST SEIZE THEM PIECE BY PIECE.

METSU!
BOOOOOOM
UGH...
SHOO
SHKKKK
YOU LITTLE BRAT!

HEY, CAN'T WE FIGHT BACK YET?
WE CAN START NOW, CAN'T WE?
?!
WHAT IS IT TALKING ABOUT?
DO WE STILL HAVE TO WAIT?
UGH ...
HUMPH!
SLITHERR
HMM ...
ITS REGENERATIVE POWER HAS BEEN IMPROVED.

GIVE ME...THE GO AHEAD...
I DON'T HAVE THE PATIENCE TO KEEP LETTING THAT KID...
KREAK
...MAKE A FOOL OUT OF ME.
KREAK
KREAK
KREAK
IT'S TRANS-FORMING VERY QUICKLY, TOO!
I THOUGHT AYAKASHI ARE ABLE TO DRAW A LOT OF POWER ONLY WHEN THEY ARE IN CLOSE PROXIMITY TO KARASUMORI, BUT...

NO NEWS HAS COME FROM THE WATCH BIRD...
THAT MEANS THAT NEITHER THE AYAKASHI THAT IS UNDERGROUND NOR THE ONE ON THE GROUND HAS TRANSFORMED YET.
THIS IS VERY INTER-ESTING.
WE MAY NEED FURTHER STUDY OF THE CORRELATION BETWEEN KEKKAI AND DISTANCE, BUT...
...THERE ARE CERTAINLY FACTORS OTHER THAN TIME THAT INFLUENCE THE EFFECT OF KARASUMORI'S POWER!
ALL RIGHT.
I'M GOING TO GIVE YOU THE GO-SIGN NOW.
SHF
ZIP

SNAAAP
THE BATTLE ...
...BEGINS NOW.

Chapter 44: White Feather Kids
WHIRR
PM PHH
CHUCKLE.
I THOUGHT WE'D HAVE TO WAIT A LITTLE LONGER.
IT LOOKS LIKE WE CAN GET STARTED.
WHOOOSH
FLINCH
KREAK

Chapter 44:
White Feather Kids
Shirahago (White Feather Kid):
This ayakashi can disassemble itself into small feathers and maneuver each feather independently as a weapon.

WHAT ?!
BAM
BAM
AW!
BAM
BAM
BAM
WSSH
HEY!
DASH
AFTER IT, HAKUBI!
I GUESS I'LL HAVE TO USE MY NEW TECHNIQUE WHEN THE AYAKASHI DROPS ITS GUARD.

EVERYTHING IS WHITE...
BAM
BAM
IT'S NOT IMPOSSIBLE TO EVADE THIS ATTACK, BUT, WITH SUCH LIMITED VISIBILITY...
...I CAN'T EVEN SEE WHERE MY OPPONENT IS.
BAM
KETSU!
PI NG
WSH

KETSU!
WHAAAM
DARN!
BOO
METSU!
OOM
ARRGH!
YOU LITTLE ...!
RUSTLE
DK DK

SHWM
SHWM
IMMEDIATE REGENERA-TION, EH?
IT DOESN'T HELP TO DESTROY IT PAR-TIALLY.
I MUST COMPLETELY OBLITERATE IT AS SOON AS IT RESTORES ITS BODILY FORM.
IT LOOKS LIKE...
...IT SUFFERS MORE DAMAGE WHEN IT ASSUMES HUMAN FORM THAN WHEN IT TURNS INTO FEATHERS.
HIZUKI!
YOUR ARM...THE KID DID THAT TO YOU?
HUMPH!
SWIK
DON'T GET IN MY WAY.
WAIT.

THE THREE OF US MUST ACT AS ONE.
YOUR ENEMY IS MINE.
RIGHT?
WE ARE ALL EQUAL.
DON'T TRY TO STAND OUT, ALL RIGHT?
WHERE DID YOU GET SO MUCH POWER?
THAT'S WHAT YOU REALLY WANT TO KNOW, ISN'T IT?
DON'T WORRY. I'LL SHARE THE POWER WITH YOU LATER.

WH
?!
AM
UGH
...
FUZUKI
!
SHK
WHAT THE HECK IS THAT? A THREE LAYERED KEKKAI?!
I WAS ONLY ABLE TO CATCH ONE...
WOOSH

METSU!
STUPID AYA-KASHISI ...

WHY ON EARTH DID THEY LINK UP SO SOON?
THEY MADE IT EASY FOR THE KEKKAISHI TO ATTACK THEM ALL AT ONCE.
THEY SHOULD HAVE USED THEIR BRAINS AND STAYED AWAY FROM EACH OTHER WHILE ACCUMULATING POWER...
A MULTI-LAYERED KEKKAI, EH?
PROBABLY REINFORCES THE KEKKAI'S RESILIENCE AND DESTRUCTIVE POWER...
YOU...
...LITTLE BRATS!
HIZUKI...
THIS...
...WAS ALL FOR NAUGHT.
I THOUGHT POWER WOULD BRING US FREEDOM...
BUT IF ANY OF US ARE LOST, THE FREEDOM WE'VE ATTAINED MEANS...
...NOTHING...
MIZUKI.
ARE YOU SAYING YOU WANT TO QUIT?

NOT AT ALL.
KREAK
MY RAGE WON'T SUBSIDE ...
KREAK KREAK
KREAK KREAK
...UNTIL THOSE BRATS ARE DEAD!
WHIRR
SHK
ARE THEY TRANS-FORMING?
SHOOT. THEIR EVIL POWER JUST INTENSIFIED!
WHIRR RR
RR
WHIRR RR

WH... WHAT THE...?!
THEY'VE JOINED TOGETHER AS ONE GIANT AYAKASHI!

FLAP
FLAAP
KYAA!
WHIRRR
WAH!
WHIRRR
WHIRRR
RUMMBLE
ARGHHH!
AUGH!
MADA-RAO!
RR
RR

WHIRR

...

FLAP

WOOSH
WOO
OSH

WSSH
WSS

KLINK

WHAM
MMMM
ZIP
ZIP
ZIP
ZIP
ZIP
ZIP

FAN-
TASTIC
!
IS THIS
THE
POWER
OF
KARA-
SUMORI?!
RUMMBLE
WOOSH
WHIRR
RR
RR
DRMM
DRMM
DRMM

HEH!
I CAN FINALLY SEE WHAT'S GOING ON...
NEXT TIME, I'M NOT GOING TO MISS.

HAOOO OOOO
Chapter 45: Tokine's Arrow
CHUCKLE ...
I DIDN'T EXPECT THE POWER OF KARASUMORI TO BE THIS AWESOME..
WELL, KEKKAISHI GUARDIANS OF KARA-SUMORI...
...WHAT WILL BE YOUR NEXT MOVE?
FWAAP

Chapter 45: Tokine's Arrow

WSSSH
HERE IT COMES!
CLENCH
...
KLINK
WHAMMM!

ZIP ZAP
ZIP ZIP
ZIP ZAP
WHIRRR
RRRR
ZIP ZAP
SHLAK
ARGHH!
ZIP ZAP ZIP ZAP ZIP ZAP ZIP ZAP
HONEY! ARE WE ALL RIGHT?
UGH!
WE'RE...
...IN BIG TROUBLE.
I MUST HOLD ON...
SNAPPP
GASP!

HUH?

YOU ALL RIGHT, TOKINE?

Y-YEAH.
HOW DID HE GET SO CLOSE TO ME?
AND HIS KEKKAI...
DID HE FEND OFF THAT POWERFUL ATTACK WITH A SINGLE KEKKAI?
NOT ONLY THAT, BUT HE STILL HAD ENOUGH POWER TO HELP ME.
TOKINE!

THE FEATHERS ARE A PART OF THAT AYAKASHI, AREN'T THEY?
I'M THINKING THE ONLY SOLUTION IS TO STRIKE IT WHEN IT REINTEGRATES ALL THE FEATHERS INTO ITS BODY.
WHAT DO YOU THINK?
I'M SURE...
...IT WILL BE THE FASTEST WAY TO TERMINATE IT.
WELL THEN.
WILL YOU HELP ME?
WSSH
WSSH
THE KEKKAISHI HAVE NARROWLY SURVIVED THE ATTACK.
I GUESS THE WINNER WILL BE DETERMINED IN THE NEXT ROUND.

WHAT A WONDERFUL PLACE THIS IS!
I CAME HERE TO CONDUCT SOME EXPERIMENTS, BUT WE MIGHT AS WELL TAKE OVER THIS PLACE TONIGHT IF EVERYTHING WORKS OUT!
WOOOOSH
I DON'T QUITE UNDERSTAND WHY OUR LEADERS HAVE BEEN SO CAUTIOUS ABOUT DEALING WITH THIS PLACE.
IT'S CLEAR THAT THE LAND WORKS TO OUR ADVANTAGE.
WHAM
SHK
UGH...
GRP
WHAT?! HOW ANNOYING!

ZK
ZK
ZK
ZK
ZK
!
WHAM
NGHH ...
WHOOM
GLARE

METSU!
I SEE...
THE GIRL'S ACCURACY ENABLES HER TO STOP THE AYAKASHI'S MOVEMENT...
...AND THEN THE BOY STRIKES IT WITH HIS AWESOME POWER.
PLIP
PLIP
FLAP
...
...
FLAP
HMPH!
THEY MAKE A GOOD TEAM...

BUT HE FAILED TO TERMINATE IT.
HE WASTED HIS ENERGY.
WITH ONLY THAT LEVEL OF DAMAGE, THE AYAKASHI WILL BE ABLE TO RESTORE ITSELF VERY QUICKLY AND...
WHAT?
YOSHI-MORI? YOUR KEKKAI HAS GROWN MORE POWERFUL, HASN'T IT?
TOKINE.
THAT AYAKASHI ASSEMBLES ALL ITS FEATHERS ...
...TO MARSHAL ITS STRENGTH BEFORE IT RESTORES ITSELF.
SHWP
LET'S ATTACK IT WHEN THAT HAPPENS.

OO
OO
OO
OO OH
OOOOOOO
SHWP
READY?
HOI!
VRR
RR
JOSO!
ZK
ZK
ZK
ZK
ZK
ZK
RMM
RMM
RMM

KETSU!
WHAT? THE KID STILL HAS THAT MUCH STRENGTH?
FLAP
FLAP
FLAP
...!
...!
FLAP

NNGH...
THAT'S RIGHT.
HUMPH.
EVEN IF IT'S ENCLOSED, IT CAN STILL OVERPOWER THE KID AND WIN THE BATTLE.
AT THIS POINT, THE GIRL DOESN'T HAVE ENOUGH POWER TO COUNT FOR MUCH.
IT'S GOING TO BE A LONG-DRAWN-OUT WAR WITH THE BOY AND THE AYAKASHI.
TOKINE!
TELL ME HOW YOU DO IT.
DO WHAT?
THE THREE-LAYERED KEKKAI!
THAT ENHANCES THE STRENGTH OF THE KEKKAI, DOESN'T IT?
...
I DON'T KNOW IF HE CAN LEARN HOW TO DO IT RIGHT AWAY...
MAYBE I SHOULD CREATE A MULTI-LAYERED KEKKAI AND SUPPORT HIM FROM THE SIDE...
BUT...I DON'T HAVE MUCH STRENGTH LEFT...
FORTUNATELY, THIS PLACE IS WORKING IN OUR FAVOR!
THAT'S NOT A GOOD TECHNIQUE FOR YOU.
WOOSH
KLINNNK

OOOOH
SHOOT!
THOSE ARROWS AGAIN...
...
ARROWS ...?
YOSHIMORI!
YOU DON'T NEED TO RESORT TO TRICKS LIKE MULTI-LAYERING KEKKAI.
JUST CONCENTRATE ON A SINGLE KEKKAI!
I'LL SUPPORT YOU FROM THE SIDE. DON'T BLOW THE TIMING, ALL RIGHT?
CHA
I UNDERSTAND WHAT YOU MEANT, GRANDMA.
KEKKAI ISN'T JUST ABOUT CAPTURING A TARGET.
CH
POWER ISN'T THE ONLY SOURCE OF STRENGTH.
MY STRONG POINT IS...
ZK
ZK
ZK
ZK
ZK
ZK

...MY
ACCURACY.
SHP
FOCUS
MY
KEKKAI...
KETSU!
ZAMMM
MMMM
...AND
PIERCE
THE
TARGET!
...?!
PING
NOW
IS
THE
TIME.

TO BE CONTINUED IN VOLUME 6!

AN EXTRA PIECE OF MANGA
ALL-OUT SPECIAL FEATURE: THE UNTOLD STORY BEHIND THE PRODUCTION OF KEKKAISHI & THE UNTOLD STORY ABOUT MY STUDIO
ANECDOTE ONE:
ABOUT THE APPEARANCE OF THE CHARACTERS
AS YOU MAY KNOW, COMIC SERIALS IN WEEKLY MAGAZINES HAVE A DEADLINE EVERY WEEK.
EVERY WEEK? THOSE DEADLINES COME TOO FREQUENTLY, DON'T THEY?
CONSEQUENTLY, ALTHOUGH I SOMETIMES WISH I HAD MORE TIME TO SPEND WORKING OUT THE PLOTS OF MY COMICS, I OFTEN HAVE TO RELY ON IMPULSES AND INTUITION.
LATERAL JUMPS (THIS IS HOW I FEEL.)
WHIMS AND QUICK THOUGHTS ARE EFFECTIVE IN THE SHORT TERM. HOWEVER, THEY CAN...
...CAUSE TROUBLE LATER ON.
WHAT AM I GOING TO DO NOW?
IF THE TROUBLE CONCERNS THE PLOTLINE, I CAN USUALLY PATCH THINGS UP AND PUT THE STORY BACK ON TRACK.
THE STORY FALLS INTO PLACE IF I DO THIS, DOESN'T IT?
HEH HEH
THE DIFFICULT THING TO CHANGE ONCE YOU'VE INTRODUCED IT?
...IS A CHARACTER'S APPEARANCE!
TANABE DRAWN AS A FISH
THE VISUAL IMPRESSION IS A KEY PART OF WHAT MAKES A CHARACTER STICK IN THE READER'S MIND. THEREFORE, IT'S ESSENTIAL TO PUT SUFFICIENT EFFORT INTO CRAFTING THE APPEARANCE OF EACH CHARACTER.
LET ME GIVE YOU AN EXAMPLE.
GO!

HE CERTAINLY LOOKED LIKE A MONSTER, AND I RETAINED THIS IMAGE OF URO UNTIL I ACTUALLY BEGAN SCRIPTING THE STORY. I ALMOST MADE A BIG MISTAKE.
HA HA HA. WHAT A WEIRD, CHUBBY GUY.
I USE A DRAWING PAD ←TO MAKE A ROUGH SKETCH OF MY CHARACTERS.
AN INITIAL IMAGE FOR LORD URO
WOW. HE'S NOT CUTE AT ALL.
I'M GLAD I CHANGED THE WAY LORD URO LOOKS.
AREN'T YOU?
EXAMPLE TWO: TANABE VS. COCKROACH
IT HAPPENED LATE AT NIGHT WHEN I HAD JUST FINISHED THE DAY'S WORK.
GUESS I'LL BRUSH MY TEETH AND GO TO BED.
HMM!
GLARE!

OH, NO!
HEY, GUYS! HELP!
MY ASSISTANTS
DK
KYAA
IT'S HUGE!
IT'S BLACK!
I SEE IT!
AREN'T ANY OF YOU BRAVE ENOUGH TO CONFRONT IT?
NO! EEP! HEE!
I'M AFRAID NO ONE IS.
COCKATIEL GOAT FLYING SQUIRREL
I HAVE NO CHOICE THEN...
THAT LITTLE INSECT!
ROLL ROLL ROLL
IT'S MY HOUSE AFTER ALL.
NEWSPAPER
THERE WAS A CREVICE THERE.
YAAH!
NEWSPAPER ROLL ATTACK!
YAH!
PLONK
SHK SHK SHK
AHHH!

SHHHF
I'LL NEVER GET IT IF I MISS AGAIN. IT'S HIDING BEHIND THE STUFF IN THE CABINET. IF I PUSH THIS THING, I MIGHT SQUASH IT. SHOULD I DO IT?
SHOULD I GO FOR IT?
IT MUST HAVE GONE INSIDE THE CABINET...
ERASERS
THE ROACH.
I'M GOING TO WRAP IT WITH LAYERS AND LAYERS OF KLEENEX!
FWP FWP
GRB
NO, THAT'S NOT ENOUGH!
GLASS (IMPACT RESISTANT)
I SHOULDN'T WIMP OUT NOW!
YEOW! I HEARD THE CRUNCH! OH MY GOSH!
UGH...
YEOW!
KRUSH
I WISH MY ASSISTANTS COULD JOIN THE BATTLE WITH ME...
WINNER: TANABE!
NOTE: USUALLY, I AM A RELATIVELY MILD-MANNERED PERSON.
TANABE-SAN!
GLASS TWIST ATTACK!!!
GYAAA!
DIE!!
SHRNCH SHRNCH
GLASS
ROACH BURIED IN LAYERS OF KLEENEX.

MESSAGE FROM YELLOW TANABE

I bought a sofa. A leather one! I like the cold feeling of the leather when I sit on it. Now I can take a nap whenever I have free time. **If** I ever have free time!

KEKKAISHI

VOLUME 5

STORY AND ART BY YELLOW TANABE

Translation/Yuko Sawada
Touch-up Art & Lettering/Stephen Dutro
Cover Design & Graphic Layout/Amy Martin
Editor/Andy Nakatani

Editor in Chief, Books/Alvin Lu
Editor in Chief, Magazines/Marc Weidenbaum
VP of Publishing Licensing/Rika Inouye
VP of Sales/Gonzalo Ferreyra
Sr. VP of Marketing/Liza Coppola
Publisher/Hyoe Narita

Printed in the U.S.A.

Published by VIZ Media, LLC
P.O. Box 77010
San Francisco, CA 94107

VIZ Media Edition
10 9 8 7 6 5 4 3 2
First printing, January 2006
Second printing, November 2007

www.viz.com

RATED

FOR TEEN

PARENTAL ADVISORY
KEKKAISHI is rated T for Teen and is recommended for ages 13 and up. It contains fantasy violence.

ratings.viz.com

store.viz.com

Editor's Recommendations

MÄR

Ginta Toramizu is a 14-year-old kid who doesn't have a lot going for him: he's near-sighted, doesn't do well in school, sucks at sports, and to top it off—he's short! Then one day a supernatural figure appears at his school and summons him to a mysterious and exciting new world! In this strange universe filled with magic and wonder, he is strong, tough, agile—and he can see without his glasses! Thus, Ginta begins a mystical quest in search of the magical items known as "ÄRMS," with his companions Jack and the talking iron-ball weapon known as "Babbo."

Fullmetal Alchemist

In an alchemical ritual gone wrong, Edward Elric lost his leg. He was lucky…his brother Alphonse lost his entire body. At the cost of his arm, Edward was able to rescue his brother's soul and preserve it in a suit of steel armor. Equipped with mechanical "auto-mail" limbs, Edward becomes a state alchemist, serving the government on deadly missions and seeking the one thing that can restore his and his brother's bodies…the legendary Philosopher's Stone.

Excel Saga

Today the city—tomorrow, the world! That's the plan of Il Palazzo, the haughty leader of ACROSS, a secret society based somewhere deep beneath the streets and sewers of Fukuoka, Japan. It's a good thing he's starting small, because ACROSS begins its bid for global domination with just two members—Il Palazzo and Excel, the teenaged girl smitten with him.

SPLORT!
THE PROOF IS IN MY SEAL!
FLASH
Tokine's Grandmother and Yoshimori's Grandfather

What's a Future

Ryo thought he was normal until he learned his arm was secretly replaced with a powerful weapon. But he soon learns that there are others—teens like him—with mechanical limbs and no idea how the weapons were implanted. Now a secret organization is after the only living samples of this technology and wants to obtain their power by any means possible...

Manga only $9.95

MEGAMAN NT WARRIOR™

Power Up Your Collections!

In the year 200X, everyone is connected to the Cyber Network and the world is a virtual utopia. But computer hacking, viruses, and high-tech crime are on the rise, creating chaos in DenTech City. Can a kid named Lan and his NetNavi MegaMan stop the madness before it destroys the world?

Manga only $7.99!

DVD only $14.98!

Manga and anime now available —buy yours today at store.viz.com!

www.megaman-ntwarrior.com

www.viz.com
store.viz.com

LOVE MANGA? LET US KNOW!

☐ Please do NOT send me information about VIZ Media products, news and events, special offers, or other information.

☐ Please do NOT send me information from VIZ Media's trusted business partners.

Name: ______________________________

Address: ______________________________

City: ________________ **State:** ________ **Zip:** ____________

E-mail: ______________________________

☐ **Male** ☐ **Female** **Date of Birth (mm/dd/yyyy):** ____/____/________ (**Under 13? Parental consent required**)

What race/ethnicity do you consider yourself? (check all that apply)

☐ White/Caucasian ☐ Black/African American ☐ Hispanic/Latino

☐ Asian/Pacific Islander ☐ Native American/Alaskan Native ☐ Other: ____________

What VIZ Media title(s) did you purchase? (indicate title(s) purchased) ____________

____

What other VIZ Media titles do you own? ____________

____

Reason for purchase: (check all that apply)

☐ Special offer ☐ Favorite title / author / artist / genre

☐ Gift ☐ Recommendation ☐ Collection

☐ Read excerpt in VIZ Media manga sampler ☐ Other ____________

Where did you make your purchase? (please check one)

☐ Comic store ☐ Bookstore ☐ Grocery Store

☐ Convention ☐ Newsstand ☐ Video Game Store

☐ Online (site:________________) ☐ Other ____________

How many manga titles have you purchased in the last year? How many were VIZ Media titles?
(ple

MA

How ... have on the titles you buy?
(ple

1 2 3 4 5

Do you purchase every volume of your favorite series?

☐ Yes! Gotta have 'em as my own ☐ No. Please explain: ______________________

What kind of manga storylines do you most enjoy? (check all that apply)

☐ Action / Adventure ☐ Science Fiction ☐ Horror
☐ Comedy ☐ Romance (shojo) ☐ Fantasy (shojo)
☐ Fighting ☐ Sports ☐ Historical
☐ Artistic / Alternative ☐ Other ______________________

If you watch the anime or play a video or TCG game from a series, how likely are you to buy the manga? (please circle, with 5 being very likely and 1 being unlikely)

1 2 3 4 5

If unlikely, please explain: ______________________

Who are your favorite authors / artists? ______________________

____

What titles would like you translated and sold in English? ______________________

____

THANK YOU! Please send the completed form to:

VIZ media™

NJW Research
42 Catharine Street
Poughkeepsie, NY 12601

Your privacy is very important to us. All information provided will be used for internal purposes only and will not be sold or otherwise divulged.